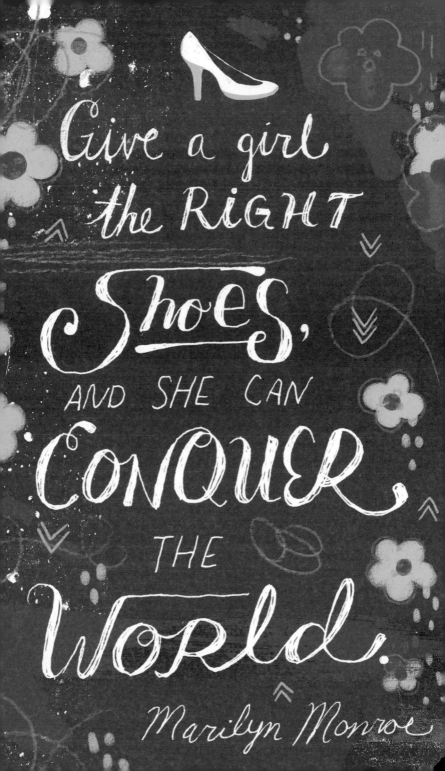

Shoes transform your
body language and attitude.
THEY LIFT YOU
physically and emotionally.
Christian Louboutin

Everyone Chases after HAPPINESS, not noticing that HAPPINESS is right at their heels.

Bertolt Brecht

THE RIGHT SHOE CAN MAKE
everything different. Jimmy Choo

I can't describe the feeling of immediate familiarity that rushed between us. The moment I clapped eyes on them I felt like I already owned them. I could only suppose that we were together in a former life.

That they were my shoes when I was a serving maid in medieval Britain or when I was a princess in ancient Egypt. Or perhaps they were the princess and I was the shoes. Who's to know? Either way I knew that we were meant to be together.

Marian Keyes

Some of them I actually realize I haven't worn. But I like to look at them.

Jenna Lyons

...sometimes,
comfort doesn't matter.

When a shoe is freakin'
fabulous,
it may be worth a subsequent
day of misery. Soak in Epsom
salts and take comfort in
the fact that you're better
than everyone else.

Clinton Kelly

I STILL HAVE MY FEET
ON THE GROUND.
I just wear better shoes.
Oprah Winfrey